STEM *trailblazer* BIOS

FACEBOOK FOUNDER AND INTERNET ENTREPRENEUR

MARK ZUCKERBERG

KARI CORNELL

Lerner Publications
Minneapolis

To all friends, old and new, with whom I've been able to connect through Facebook

Lerner Publications Company
A division of Lerner Publishing Group, Inc.
241 First Avenue North
Minneapolis, MN 55401 USA

For reading levels and more information, look up this title at www.lernerbooks.com.

Content Consultant: Martin Grider, software engineer

Library of Congress Cataloging-in-Publication Data

Cornell, Kari, author.
    Facebook founder and Internet entrepreneur Mark Zuckerberg / Kari Cornell.
        pages cm. — (STEM trailblazer bios)
    Includes bibliographical references and index.
    ISBN 978-1-4677-9527-2 (lb : alk. paper) — ISBN 978-1-4677-9715-3 (pb : alk. paper) — ISBN 978-1-4677-9716-0 (eb pdf)
    1. Zuckerberg, Mark, 1984—-Juvenile literature. 2. Facebook (Firm)—Juvenile literature. 3. Facebook (Electronic resource)—Juvenile literature. 4. Online social networks—Juvenile literature. 5. Webmasters—United States—Biography—Juvenile literature. 6. Businessmen—United States—Biography—Juvenile literature. I. Title.
    HM743.F33Z84289 2016
    302.30285—dc23   2015026147

Manufactured in the United States of America
1 – PC – 12/31/15

The images in this book are used with the permission of: © Udit Kulshrestha/Bloomberg via Getty Images, p. 4; © Bill Bertram/Wikimedia Commons (CC 2.5), p. 5; © iStockphoto.com/ DenisTangneyJr, p. 6; Seth Poppel Yearbook Library, p. 7; Sherry Tesler/Polaris/Newscom, p. 8; © Marcio Silva/Dreamstime.com, p. 10; © iStockphoto.com/Christopher Futcher, p. 12; © Rick Friedman/Corbis, p. 14; AP Photo/Charles Krupa, p. 15; AP Photo/Paul Sakuma, p. 16; © Juana Arias/The Washington Post/Getty Images, p. 17; © Justine Hunt/The Boston Globe/Getty Images, p. 18; © Juana Arias/The Boston Globe/Getty Images, p. 20; © Aerial Archives/Alamy, p. 22; Jim Wilson/The New York Times/Rex USA, p. 23; © Justin Sullivan/Getty Images, p. 24; AP Photo/L.G. Patterson, p. 25; © Zef Nikolla/Facebook/Bloomberg/Getty Images, p. 26; EPN/Newscom, p. 27.

Front cover: Joan Cros/NurPhoto/REX USA (Mark Zuckerberg), © iStockphoto.com/gmutlu (facebook screen).

Main body text set in Adrianna Regular 13/22. Typeface provided by Chank.

CONTENTS

Mark Zuckerberg discusses the need for Internet access at a conference in October 2014.

GROWING
UP

From a very young age, Mark Elliot Zuckerberg had a knack for computers. Like many other kids, he loved to play video games. But Mark also liked to program computers. When he was only twelve years old, Mark created a **software** program he called ZuckNet. ZuckNet allowed people on the same computer **network** to send one another notes instantly. Mark's father, Edward Zuckerberg, used it in his dental office, and the Zuckerberg family used it to communicate at home.

ZuckNet was the first time Mark used computers to connect people, but it wouldn't be the last. Years later, Mark would develop a social networking website called Facebook. The site, which allows friends to connect by sharing photos, stories, and videos, has become more popular than Mark or anyone else ever imagined.

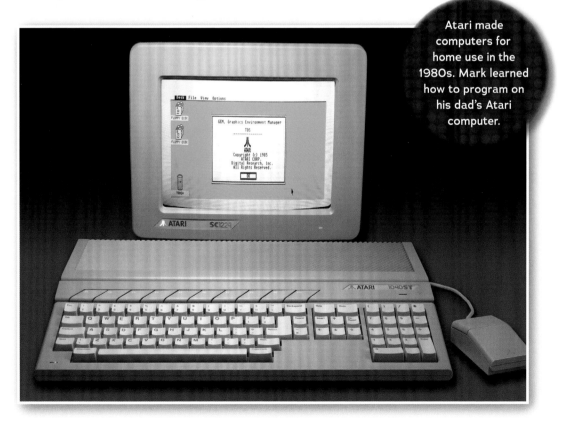

Atari made computers for home use in the 1980s. Mark learned how to program on his dad's Atari computer.

Mark was born
in White Plains,
New York.

EARLY YEARS

Mark was born in White Plains, New York, on May 14, 1984. He grew up in the small town of Dobbs Ferry, where his father was a dentist who saw patients in an office attached to the family home. Mark's mother, Karen, stayed home to take care of him; his older sister, Randi; and his two younger sisters, Donna and Arielle.

Mark spent a lot of time on the computer when he was a kid. Often instead of playing video games, Mark and his friends would create their own. Mark had many friends who loved to draw, so they would come over and draw pictures. Then Mark would use those pictures to create games.

Mark's parents could see that their son was naturally talented in computer programming. Around the age of twelve, Mark began taking a graduate-level computer class at a nearby college. On his first day, though, the instructor thought Mark's dad was the student—not him!

Edward Zuckerberg encouraged his son's interest in computers as a teenager.

Mark poses for a portrait in 2005 with his mom, dad, and two of his sisters, Randi (left) and Arielle (right).

HIGH SCHOOL

Mark attended high school at Phillips Exeter Academy in New Hampshire. When he wasn't studying or fencing, Mark could usually be found in front of his computer screen, writing **code** and developing software. As a high school senior, he worked with a friend to create a music-sharing software program that was similar to today's Pandora. The program, called Synapse, attracted the attention of Microsoft. Before Mark graduated from Exeter, Microsoft offered to buy the program and give Mark a job. But he declined the offer. Mark was young, but he already sensed that he wouldn't be happy working for someone else.

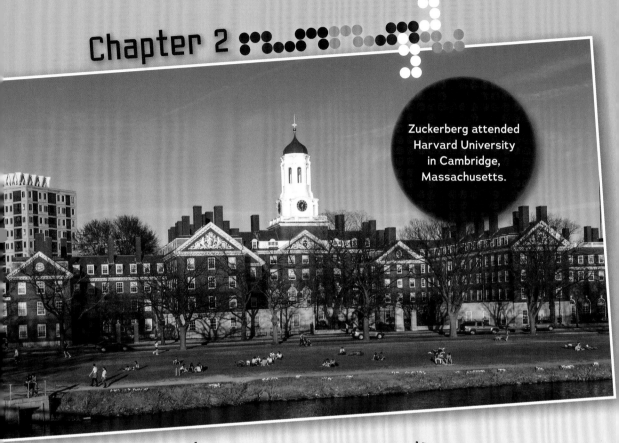

Chapter 2

Zuckerberg attended Harvard University in Cambridge, Massachusetts.

OFF TO HARVARD

In fall 2002, Zuckerberg enrolled at Harvard University, where he studied computer science and psychology. Between studying for tests and writing papers, Zuckerberg spent his time programming. Word spread quickly across campus that Zuckerberg had developed a program that

Microsoft had wanted to buy. He became known as the best software developer at the college.

During his first few weeks at Harvard, Zuckerberg created a basic software program called CourseMatch. The program allowed students to look up the classes their friends had selected. Soon after, hundreds of students were using the program to register for classes. It was exciting for Zuckerberg to see students using his program and liking it.

FACEMASH

In late October 2003, Zuckerberg developed another program. He created a website where people saw two photos of Harvard students side by side. Other students clicked a button to vote for who was more attractive. Although the site proved to be quite popular, it would eventually land Zuckerberg in hot water.

Zuckerberg created the site, called Facemash, in response to an argument with a woman. Saying he needed a distraction, he began coding at about 8 p.m. on a Saturday night and worked until the early morning hours. He enlisted the help and ideas of some of his roommates. One even provided passwords to access photos on student housing websites. Zuckerberg gathered other photos by **hacking** into the school's student files. Late in the afternoon on a Sunday in early November, Zuckerberg went live with the site. He sent the **link** to a handful of friends, and by 10 p.m., 450 students had visited Facemash. The site's popularity was more than Zuckerberg's laptop computer could handle, and it eventually froze up.

However, some student groups on campus claimed that the site was promoting sexism. The majority of the photos that appeared on Facemash when viewers were asked to choose who was better looking were photos of women. The school's

Zuckerberg's programs gave students a chance to find and share information with friends.

TECH TALK

"Hackers believe that something can always be better, and that nothing is ever complete. They just have to go fix it—often in the face of people who say it's impossible or are content with the status quo. . . . There's a hacker mantra that you'll hear a lot around Facebook offices: 'Code wins arguments.'"

—*Mark Zuckerberg*

computer services department shut down Zuckerberg's web access at 10:30 p.m. The next day, Zuckerberg and two other students who had helped him were called before Harvard's disciplinary board. The other two got off without punishment, but Zuckerberg was put on probation and required to see a counselor.

Although Zuckerberg was nearly kicked out of school for creating the Facemash website, he had gained recognition among his classmates. And he was clearly able to create websites and programs that his peers liked and wanted to use. This would serve him well later on.

Zuckerberg discusses programming with his friend Chris Hughes in May 2004.

THE FACEBOOK
IS BORN

Zuckerberg's Facemash site caught the attention of Harvard students Divya Narendra, Cameron Winklevoss, and Tyler Winklevoss. The three approached Zuckerberg in November 2003 and asked for his help creating a dating and socializing site called the Harvard Connection. Narendra and twin brothers Cameron and Tyler paid Zuckerberg to develop the site, which would provide a place for Harvard students to meet online.

Zuckerberg worked on the Harvard Connection project for a couple of months before he decided to step aside. He had other ideas he wanted to develop, and he didn't have time to do it all. Almost immediately Zuckerberg and his friends Dustin Moskovitz, Chris Hughes, and Eduardo Saverin began work on their own version of a social networking site. They called the project Thefacebook.

Tyler Winklevoss (*left*), Divya Narendra (*center*), and Cameron Winklevoss asked Zuckerberg to develop a dating website for Harvard students.

home   search   global   social net   invite   faq   logout

Mark Zuckerberg's Profile

Puget Sound

Picture

Information

Account Info:

Name: Mark Zuckerberg

Member Since: The beginning (February 4, 2004)

Last Update: July 19, 2005

Basic Info:

School

Status:

Sex:

Residence

Send Mark a Message

Poke Him!

Zuckerberg named his new social networking site Thefacebook.

Based on the idea of Harvard's printed facebooks—which were student directories featuring names and photos of those attending Harvard—the site would include photos of its members. But unlike the printed versions, the online facebook let its members create their own personal page. They could post information about themselves, **upload** photos, and connect and talk with other friends who were also on the site. Most important, members could use **privacy settings** to control who could view their page. Zuckerberg didn't think of the site as a way to meet potential dates, as the Harvard Connection was to be. Instead, the site provided users with a way to share information about themselves with friends they already knew. It was a digital way to socialize that also provided a map of each member's network of friends.

LESSONS LEARNED

Zuckerberg had learned a few lessons from the Facemash experience, so he made some changes this time around. First, he followed the advice of an article in the *Harvard Crimson* newspaper. The article suggested that Facemash wouldn't have run into quite so many problems if Zuckerberg had simply allowed students to upload their own photos instead of snagging them from university networks. This gave members control over their own personal information. Second, rather

Thefacebook website let students create a personal profile and upload photos to their page. Students could also decide who was allowed to view their page.

than using the university network as he had with Facemash, Zuckerberg paid another company to use their network. This gave Zuckerberg plenty of space to host the site. It also meant that if it became wildly popular, Thefacebook could easily move beyond Harvard University.

GOING LIVE

On February 4, 2004, Thefacebook went live. Zuckerberg launched the site by sending the link to his friends at his dorm, called Kirkland House, and asking them to join and invite their friends. Within five days, nearly one thousand people

As Thefacebook grew at Harvard, Zuckerberg and Dustin Moskovitz *(left)* began planning how to offer the site to other universities.

had signed up. By the end of the first week, about half of the university had an account on Thefacebook. And after only three weeks, the site had six thousand users.

While Thefacebook was continuing to grow at Harvard, Zuckerberg's roommate Dustin Moskovitz began working to offer the site at other Ivy League schools. The site was launched at Columbia on February 25, at Stanford on February 26, and at Yale on February 29. Then Thefacebook became available at Cornell and Dartmouth on March 7. By the end of March, the site had more than thirty thousand members.

Chapter 4

Thefacebook attracted thousands of users at more than thirty colleges to its site in 2004.

GROWTH AND THE
MOVE WEST

While it was exciting to see Thefacebook catch on so quickly, it was becoming a challenge to maintain the site. Each time new users joined, Zuckerberg and Moskovitz had to rework the site to keep it running smoothly. Sometimes they needed to add more main computers, called servers, to store the additional user information. And Zuckerberg, Moskovitz, Hughes, and Saverin were all still taking a full load of college courses. This often meant long nights spent juggling homework and site upkeep.

As the spring semester ended in 2004, Zuckerberg made the difficult decision to leave Harvard to turn Thefacebook into a business and become an entrepreneur. Zuckerberg thought Thefacebook had the potential to grow well beyond the current membership of thirty-four colleges. He also wanted to live in an area where he'd have connections to other new technology companies.

TECH TALK

"[Facebook] is shaping the broader web. . . . The story of social networking has really been about getting . . . people connected. . . . I think that the story that people are going to remember five years from now isn't how this one site was built; it was how every single service that you use is now going to be better with your friends."

—Mark Zuckerberg

In June 2004, Zuckerberg officially moved Thefacebook
west to Palo Alto, California. Zuckerberg, Moskovitz, and two
other **programmers** rented a four-bedroom house, which
also served as Thefacebook offices. By the end of the year,
Thefacebook had one million users, but they didn't get there
without a few growing pains.

UPS AND DOWNS OF SUCCESS

Throughout the early years of unbelievable growth,
Thefacebook experienced some challenges. Perhaps the
biggest setback happened in September 2004, when Harvard
Connection creators Divya Narendra, Cameron Winklevoss,

and Tyler Winklevoss sued Zuckerberg for stealing their idea for a social website. Rather than face a lengthy court case, Zuckerberg decided to settle a few years later.

Around the same time, Zuckerberg wanted to grow Thefacebook with the help of his friend Sean Parker. Parker found people he knew in the tech industry who were interested in giving Thefacebook money in exchange for voting shares in the company (or a say in how the company is run). Unfortunately, this caused a falling out between Zuckerberg and his former Harvard classmate Eduardo Saverin. Saverin also sued Zuckerberg in 2005.

Sean Parker *(right)* with Zuckerberg and Moskovitz *(center)* at Thefacebook headquarters in Palo Alto in May 2005

Zuckerberg speaks to developers about Facebook's new features at a conference in April 2010.

FACEBOOK'S
SUCCESS

Despite the setbacks, Thefacebook grew rapidly. Zuckerberg knew that he would need more money for new computer equipment to keep up with demand. An investor gave Thefacebook a loan for $500,000, and more investors soon followed. In September 2005, the company dropped the *the* from its name and became known as just *Facebook*.

Zuckerberg promised the investors that he would continue to grow Facebook. By introducing Facebook to more colleges and to high schools, Zuckerberg and Moskovitz were able to increase membership to 5.5 million by the end of 2005.

Meanwhile, other companies were beginning to take notice of Zuckerberg's success. In July 2006, Yahoo offered to buy Facebook for $1 billion. Zuckerberg turned down the deal, however. He had a goal for Facebook, and he was determined to make it happen under his ownership. Zuckerberg's dream was to connect everyone in the world through Facebook.

In 2005, the Facebook site was updated with a new name, logo, and design.

In September 2006, he took one giant step toward this goal by making the site available to anyone over the age of thirteen who had an e-mail address.

GOING PUBLIC

In the years since, Facebook has become one of the most widely recognized companies in the world. On May 18, 2012, Zuckerberg decided to put the site's popularity to the test. For the first time, anyone could buy shares in Facebook. They first sold for around $38. By June 2015, the company was selling for $82 per share.

Zuckerberg and employees celebrate the announcement that Facebook will start selling shares on May 18, 2012.

Facebook continues to add new users every day. As of March 2015, there were 1.4 billion active monthly Facebook users. Zuckerberg and his team are constantly updating the network, adding new features, and looking for ways to increase Facebook's appeal and the company's profits.

And in late July 2015, Zuckerberg announced some exciting personal news. He shared that he and his wife are expecting their first child. Naturally, he made the announcement on his Facebook page—so his 25 million followers all found out at once!

In July 2015, Zuckerberg and his wife, Priscilla, announced that they were expecting a baby girl.

Just ten years ago, mass announcements on a social networking website weren't even possible. So how will Zuckerberg change how we communicate in the next ten years? How will you use Facebook to share your next newsworthy moment with the world?

TECH TALK

"At Facebook, we're inspired by technologies that have revolutionized how people spread and consume information. We often talk about inventions like the printing press and the television—by simply making communication more efficient, they led to a complete transformation of many important parts of society. They gave more people a voice. . . . They brought us closer together."

—*Mark Zuckerberg*

TIMELINE

1984
Mark Elliot Zuckerberg is born in White Plains, New York, on May 14.

1996
Twelve-year-old Mark creates ZuckNet, a messaging software program.

2001
Zuckerberg develops Synapse around this time. Microsoft eventually shows interest in buying this music-sharing software program.

2002
While attending Harvard University, Zuckerberg develops a software program called CourseMatch.

2003
Zuckerberg creates the program Facemash. Afterward, Harvard students Divya Narendra, Cameron Winklevoss, and Tyler Winklevoss ask Zuckerberg to create Harvard Connection, a school dating site.

2004
Zuckerberg's Thefacebook website goes live. Harvard Connection creators sue Zuckerberg for allegedly stealing their idea. Zuckerberg leaves Harvard and moves to Palo Alto, California, to focus full-time on Thefacebook.

2005
An investor gives $500,000 to Facebook. The site has 5.5 million members.

2006
Zuckerberg declines Yahoo's offer to buy Facebook for $1 billion.

2012
Facebook shares are made available for sale to the public.

2015
Facebook has 1.4 billion active monthly users.

SOURCE NOTES

9 Jessica Guynn, "Mark Zuckerberg on Oculus, Diversity, Birthdays and Onsies," *USA Today*, May 15, 2015, http://www.usatoday.com/story/tech/2015/05/14/mark-zuckerberg-town-hall-oculus-diversity-birthdays-ukraine-onesies/27344599.

13 "Mark Zuckerberg's Letter to Investors: 'The Hacker Way,'" *Wired*, February 1, 2012, http://www.wired.com/2012/02/zuck-letter.

19 Jason Fell, "On Facebook's 10th Birthday, Mark Zuckerberg Reflects on the Long Journey of Creating a Social Media Powerhouse," *Entrepreneur*, February 4, 2014, http://www.entrepreneur.com/article/231256.

21 Mark Zuckerberg, "Exclusive Interview with Facebook Leadership: Mark Zuckerberg, CEO/Co-Founder & Sheryl Sandberg, COO," interview by Charlie Rose, *Charlie Rose*, PBS, November 6, 2011, http://www.charlierose.com/watch/60001374.

28 "Mark Zuckerberg's Letter to Investors," *Wired*.

GLOSSARY

code
a set of instructions for a computer program

hacking
the process of figuring out passwords and accessing information saved on private computers

link
an address to a specific website on the Internet

network
a group of two or more computers linked together

privacy settings
features that users can select to control what others can view on a web page

programmers
people who write computer code or create computer programs

software
a set of instructions that direct a computer to perform certain tasks

upload
to move content, such as photographs or videos, from a personal computer to a website

FURTHER INFORMATION

BOOKS

DiPiazza, Francesca Davis. *Friend Me! 600 Years of Social Networking in America*. Minneapolis: Twenty-First Century Books, 2012. Learn about the history of social networking, from telegrams to Facebook.

McCue, Camille. *Coding for Kids for Dummies*. Hoboken, NJ: John Wiley & Sons, 2015. Learn the basics of writing your own computer code and developing simple software.

Minton, Eric. *Social Networking and Social Media Safety*. New York: PowerKids, 2014. This book provides helpful tips for staying safe while visiting and using social media sites.

WEBSITES

Facebook Newsroom
http://newsroom.fb.com
Visit the official Facebook website for the latest news and statistics about the site.

Kidz Social
http://www.kidzsocial.com
Check out this social networking site that's just for kids!

Mark Zuckerberg's Facebook Page
https://www.facebook.com/zuck
Follow Mark Zuckerberg on Facebook, where he gives updates on the latest Facebook features.

LERNER

SOURCE™

Expand learning beyond the printed book. Download free, complementary educational resources for this book from our website, www.lerneresource.com.

INDEX

ABOUT THE AUTHOR

Kari Cornell is a freelance writer and editor who lives with her husband, two sons, and dog in Minneapolis, Minnesota. One of her favorite things to do is to write about people who've found a way to do what they love. When she's not writing, she likes tinkering in the garden, cooking, and making something clever out of nothing. Learn more about her work at karicornell.wordpress.com.